WHY DOLPHINS CALL

A Story of Dionysus

Retold by Jamie and Scott Simons ▪ *Pictures by Deborah Winograd*

Silver Press

Published by Silver Press, a division of Silver Burdett Press, Inc.
Simon & Schuster, Inc., Prentice Hall Bldg., Englewood Cliffs, NJ 07632.
Printed in the United States of America.
10 9 8 7 6 5 4 3 2

Art Director: Linda Huber

Library of Congress Cataloging-in-Publication Data
Simons, Jamie.
Why dolphins call : a story of Dionysus / retold by Jamie and
Scott Simons; pictures by Deborah Winograd.
p.   cm.—(The Gods of Olympus)
Summary: Kidnapped by pirates, young Dionysus turns his cold
-hearted captors into friendly dolphins.
1. Dionysus (Greek deity)—Juvenile literature. 1. Dionysus
(Greek deity) 2. Mythology, Greek.] I. Simons, Scott.
II. Winograd, Deborah, ill. III. Title. IV. Series: Simons, Jamie.
Gods of Olympus.
BL820.B2S55 1991
292.2′113—dc20   89-49531
ISBN 0-671-69125-2   ISBN 0-671-69121-X (lib. bdg.)   CIP
AC

IN ANCIENT GREECE, Zeus sat on his throne on a mountain so high it touched the heavens. But the king of the gods was not alone. Many gods and goddesses lived with Zeus at the peak of Mount Olympus.

They sat at the top of the world, watching people on earth. "Many are living good lives and obeying our laws," Zeus said to the others. "We must reward them."

So the gods gave great gifts. They showed people how to grow onions, tomatoes, and lemons. They filled the seas with sardines, oysters, and shrimp. Dionysus, the son of Zeus, taught people to grow grapes and make sweet wine.

But all was not happy on earth. Some people did not live by the laws of the gods. They rode in great ships and stole from others. These thieves of the sea were called pirates.

One day a band of pirates sailed by a small, rocky island with a white sand beach. Being pirates, they had sharp eyes. Through a grove of lazy palm trees, they spied a boy, asleep on the beach.

"Look!" yelled a sailor from high on the ship's mast. "The boy is wearing royal robes of gold and purple."

"Ah ha!" cackled the pirate king. "He must be a prince. We will take the boy and hold him for ransom. Surely his family will pay many gold coins to get him back."

While the boy slept, the pirates gently lifted him onto the ship. The boat rocked softly in the waves and the boy never stirred.

Quickly, the pirates put out to sea. Some climbed the tall mast and set the sails to catch the wind. Others rowed. Soon the great ship was speeding through the water.

Feeling the rush of wind on his face, the boy opened his eyes. His rocky island was now just a tiny speck in the distance. He looked around the boat. Stolen treasure and weapons covered the deck.

"This is a pirate ship!" said the boy. "I must pretend I do not know."

Seeing the boy awake, the pirate king strolled over to him. "Your royal highness, you are so lucky we found you," said the pirate in his sweetest voice. "From your royal robes we knew you were a prince. Surely, your father, the king, will miss you. Let us take you home to him. Which island does he rule?"

"My father lives on a mountain so high it touches the heavens," smiled the boy. "But don't bother yourself. I was not on my way home. You see, I travel from place to place, teaching people how to grow grapes and make wine. Just take me back to the rocky island and I will be fine."

The pirate king smiled and winked at his crew.

"Of course," he laughed. "We will be happy to take you back to the island."

But he did not turn around. Instead, he steered far out to sea toward the setting sun.

When the stars came out, the boy saw that the ship was heading in the wrong direction. He knew the pirates had lied.

Now the boy stood boldly before the pirate king and spoke with anger.

"You are fools to lie to me. I grew up with tigers and leopards more bloodthirsty than you. I am no ordinary boy. I am Dionysus, son of the great god Zeus."

The pirates laughed, thinking the boy was bluffing.

"If Zeus is your father," they snickered, "let him throw lightning bolts to crush us."

"Yes," howled the pirate king. "At least, have him blow a few rounds of thunder our way!"

Now the pirates rowed even harder, sending the ship farther out
to sea.

"Soon we will live like kings," they shouted.

"Soon we will need bigger vessels to carry all our gold," laughed
the pirate king.

But suddenly the smiles froze on their lips.

Though the pirates rowed with all their might, the ship would not
move. It had stopped dead, stuck in the mighty sea.

Waves rolled over the deck, as the small boy grew taller than the mast. Grape vines wound wildly around the ship. Blood-red wine dripped down the white sail. The pirate king's eyes popped wide open.

In place of the boy stood the god Dionysus. He wore a crown of leaves and held an ivy staff. The bright ghosts of tigers and leopards stood beside him. They bared their teeth and growled angrily at the pirates.

"Help!" yelled the pirates as they jumped into the sea.
Many could not swim. They splashed wildly in the water,
gasping for air. Huge waves crashed over them.

"You have lived evil lives," said Dionysus grimly. "But to show you my greatness, I will not let you drown. Instead, you will spend the rest of your lives in the sea."

Instantly, the wicked pirates felt their arms grow small. Their hands turned to flippers. Their legs grew together into one great fan-shaped tail.

Then the men felt their skin turn slippery and watched one another's faces grow long until...

the pirates had turned into a school of dolphins.

Happy to be alive in any form, the dolphins called to each other.

"From this day on," proclaimed Dionysus, "you will be friends to all who travel the seas. You will guide anyone in danger who needs your help."

Even today, dolphins guide sailors lost in dark sea waters.

"Come this way and follow us," they seem to call.

Then just as Dionysus promised, they lead the sailors safely home.